# On The Road To Enlightenment

**Sharlene Sema Raston**

*'If we focus on what ignites the greatness in a person, the messenger becomes irrelevant. It is hard in our culture that has an inherit way of adoring and focusing on the persona and not the message'.*

Unknown

# Contents

Introduction .......................................................................... 1

CHAPTER 1: An Introduction to Buddhism ...................... 2

CHAPTER 2: Human Nature ............................................ 11

CHAPTER 3: Work as Play ............................................... 16

CHAPTER 4: Social Media ............................................... 21

CHAPTER 5: Mental Masturbation .................................. 24

CHAPTER 6: Rational Emotive Behavioural Therapy in a Nutshell ................................................................................ 28

Chapter 7: The Model of Emotional Disturbance ............ 33

Chapter 8: The Sociopath World ...................................... 36

chapter 9: The Story about the Fisherman ....................... 47

Chapter 10: The Beauty of Silence ................................... 50

CHAPTER 11: Kopan Monastery Experience .................. 52

Chapter 12: Food for Thought .......................................... 55

Chapter 13: Playing the Game of Life ............................. 57

CHAPTER 14: What Do I Believe in? ............................. 59

CHAPTER 15: The Self .................................................... 62

Chapter 16: Do Humans Really Care as Much as They Say They Do? ............................................................................. 65

CHAPTER 17: The Need to Belong ................................. 69

CHAPTER 18: Our Nature ................................................ 73

Chapter 19: My Experience as a Therapist ...................... 82

Chapter 20: Religion and Religious Beliefs ..................... 87

CHAPTER 21: Self-Reflections ........................................97
Conclusion..................................................................104
Biography ..................................................................106
Acknowledgments .....................................................109

## Introduction

Anyone who has been on a spiritual journey and goes through a stage of enlightenment normally brings something back. An enlightened person is someone who has awakened, who has discovered the secret behind all of life – all of the things we are greatly concerned about in life are indeed a big act. So once someone discovers this knowledge and reaches a stage of awakening, he or she can choose between two paths: to become a 'private Buddha', who doesn't share this knowledge, or a bodhisattva. A private Buddha goes on to ecstasy and is never seen again, whereas a bodhisattva returns to the world, appearing in the everyday world and playing by the rules of the everyday world, but now bearing *upaya*. This means the bodhisattva finds a way of showing others that he or she has been on a journey and returned – and that he or she is going to let you in on the secret too, if you wish, and play it cool while joining the everyday lives of everyday people.

I shall consider myself a bodhisattva, and this book shall be one of the instruments I have chosen to share my message.

*Sharlene Sema Raston*

# CHAPTER 1

# An Introduction to Buddhism

The philosopher Alan Watts once stated that Buddhism should not be seen as a religion but as a form of therapy, and I could not agree more with this statement.

Siddhartha Gautama, the Buddha, dedicated his whole life to finding the cause of suffering and how to cease it. I am extremely grateful that I came across his teachings because from the moment I started learning about the dharma I began an amazing journey to enlightenment – and now I will let you in on the secret, too.

Dharma can be described as any inner method that helps us overcome our grasping, our attachment, our clinging attitudes and minds, and our hatred, anger, close-mindedness and ignorance. These are poisonous to the mind because they make us restless, unhappy, and dissatisfied whenever they arise. Dharma is the method of removing them or at least to reducing them to a level where we can live with them but they don't disturb our mind. Buddha dharma is all about training the mind, mental education, and developing the mind. We all understand that these poisonous thoughts are not good for us, but we don't understand how to work with them, how to overcome them, or how to reduce them. The beauty of the Buddhist tradition is that there are so many methods—there is no shortage of methods to help us develop our mind and truly develop our human potential, our wisdom and compassion.

*This is what the path of Dharma is like. It's not that you have to do all the practices. It is sufficient to take just one of them, whichever one you really have an affinity with, and through practicing that one alone, for the rest of your life, you will achieve enlightenment. Whichever practice you choose doesn't matter; they are all valid methods for achieving enlightenment – if you practice. The key is to practice with diligence for the rest of your life.*

– Dhomang Yanthang.

In 2012, while I was working in the corporate environment as a communications manager, I went through a stage of being very unhappy, unfulfilled, and empty—and all of the pleasures in life did not fill the emptiness. I could say that I had everything I needed to be happy but anything I chased with the intention of finding fulfilment led nowhere. One odd day I had a dream. I dreamed that I was somewhere in the world in a monastery and I felt peace there. I gave importance to the dream. I shared it with one of my colleagues at work, and we decided to research where this place could be. We didn't know where to start, so we searched on Google for the area with the largest Tibetan community and the country of Nepal came up. I had never heard of Nepal before, but I started searching for monasteries there and found the Kopan Monastery. I was lucky that it had an upcoming retreat, 'Discovering Buddhism', one month later, and I registered, packed my bag, and went for the adventure. It was the first time in my life that I travelled alone, not to mention to a place I never heard of, but it felt right and my instincts kept reassuring me that everything would be fine. It was one of the best experiences of my life. Unfortunately words will not do justice to describe my first exposure to the Buddhist teachings, which I remain deeply in love with today.

Once at Kopan Monastery, I was sitting outside and chatting to a friend when a Himalayan monk approached us and we shared some ideas. He told us that we were young and obviously wanted to have fun—and that we should have fun. But the only thing we should do every day was to take five minutes to reflect about our day, what we had done, and if we were content with our actions and what to improve upon.

He spoke to us in an inspiring way. He accepted our ideas about life and our religious views. All he said was, 'If you have analysed it and it makes sense to you, it's okay. The truth is in your mind'. He highlighted the importance of reading and listening, to analysing all the teachings and only grasping what made sense to our mind. This is what the Buddha taught—not to believe in something because he said so, but because it makes rational sense to us. The Buddha said that you should burn any teaching that did not make rational sense to you as it was not made for you. He also said that we should constantly test our beliefs and guard against blind faith.

According to the monk, we should also respect our mother and love her unconditionally, but as he continued to speak he told us that all sentient beings are our mother—and therefore we should love all sentient beings. He told us the only work that has an end is the work of becoming enlightened. Once you are enlightened, you have reached the peak of wisdom and you cannot go back. You experience the ultimate joy and clarity, the state the Shakyamuni Buddha achieved—nirvana.

So why I am mentioning this? Because it is important that you do not take as the ultimate truth every single idea I share in this book, but that you analyse each idea critically to know where you stand. The best way to actually understand what we believe in, our perspective and truth, is through debate with people who do not necessarily agree with us. I challenge you to practice this and to remember that the truth is in your mind.

Let me start with a brief summary of who the Buddha was. Siddhartha Gautama was born in Nepal in the sixth century. He was a prince who lived inside the walls of a stunning palace until his twenties when he decided to go and see 'the world'. His dad had protected him from the world and its suffering, trying his best to make sure that Siddhartha was never exposed to it.

It is believed that when Siddhartha was born, a great master prophesised to the king that his son would be a great teacher and strong influence throughout the world. The king was not very happy with this prophecy, as he wanted his son to be a king. The master also shared that sadly his mother would die very early and not be able to witness her son's journey. Both prophecies came true: not long after Siddhartha was born, his mother became ill and died, and, as a result, he was raised by his aunt. Siddhartha married early in his life and had a son, too.

One day Siddhartha was adamant about seeing the world– what was outside the walls of the palace. And he did go, and what he encountered were people who were very sick. He witnessed people being cremated. He witnessed a lot of suffering, which touched him deeply.

Shocked, he went home and made the decision to leave his family, the comfort of his home, and all his wealth, and put on a robe and search for answers. He left the palace without saying goodbye; he left his newborn child and wife, too, in his quest for enlightenment. His purpose was to find the cause of suffering and how to free humanity from it. He meditated for many years at a tree, the Bodhi tree in India. He hardly ate, didn't bath, and meditated until he reached enlightenment. He basically took meditation to the extreme until one day a musician was passing by and Siddhartha overheard him saying:

'If you make the string too tight, it will break. If you make the string too loose, it will not play'. Siddhartha had an 'aha!' moment. He felt he had finally found the wisdom he was looking for: the middle path. The answer was not to live a lavish lifestyle nor the bare–boned survival of the ascetics, but somewhere in the middle. He had decided on the path to nirvana and decided to start teaching. The Buddha's first teaching was called **The Four Noble Truths**:

- Everything in life is suffering and sorrow.
- The cause of all suffering is people's selfish desire for the temporary pleasures of the world.
- The way to end all suffering is to end all desires.
- The way to overcome such desires and attain enlightenment (nirvana) is to follow the eightfold path, which is called the middle way between desire and self–denial.

The Buddha suggested that people stop working toward the short-lived pleasures of the world and the flesh and instead focus on eternal peace and nirvana through the practice of meditation and the control of impulses. It is interesting that ridding ourselves of our desires leads to less suffering; however, we can get to a point at which we desire not to desire, which is still desiring.

*Sharlene Sema Raston*

The **Eightfold Path** is a guide for achieving enlightenment, which includes:

*Panna (wisdom/insight)*

- Right understanding: knowing the truth of the four noble truths

- Right view/thought: having the urge to follow the path and reach nirvana *Sila* (ethics)

- Right speech: avoiding lying and slandering – not saying things that are unkind

- Right conduct: no killing, stealing, or being unchaste or drunk

- Right livelihood: choosing an occupation that serves humanity and does not harm life

*Samadhi (mental discipline)*

- Right effort: having self-control, especially over your thoughts, and striving for the good

- Right awareness: having psychological insight into your own motives and deeds; not being moved by either sorrow or joy

- Right concentration: pondering deeply and meditating until you experience nirvana

In addition to that, there are five precepts:

- Refrain from destroying living creatures

- Refrain from taking that which is not given
- Refrain from sexual misconduct
- Refrain from incorrect speech
- Refrain from intoxicating drinks and drugs, which lead to carelessness

There is a very powerful mantra that is recited continuously by Buddhist practitioners: *'Om Mani Pad Me Hum'*. This mantra summarises all of Buddha's teachings in one. Some believe that reciting it frequently may also contribute to achieving enlightenment. I like to summarise it by saying, 'the lotus flower grows in the mud', which means that, regardless of how toxic our environment is, we can still flourish beautifully like the beautiful lotus flower.

Buddhism places a great focus on death – the acceptance of death and how to live a life in preparation for death. It preaches reincarnation and the ultimate purpose of leaving the cycle of samsara (this world), and how we can achieve this through enlightenment.

By removing desire, by removing expectations of any sort and understanding the impermanence of everything in life certainly aids in leading a serene and calm life. However, the wish not to desire may easily become a vicious circle because once we understand the importance of eliminating our desires, we shall start desiring not to desire.

*Sharlene Sema Raston*

Some Buddhist practitioners would spend a considerate amount of time making mandala art with sand, focusing on every single detail. Once they finish the beautiful art, they destroy the work with their hands. This exercise is normally done to practice understanding the impermanence of everything. The demand for permanence in every area of our existence is the cause of human misery because there is no such thing as permanence at all.

I will elaborate on impermanence in a later chapter. My aim here has been to give you a brief overview of the perspective and teachings I enjoy and have found extremely helpful in reducing suffering.

# CHAPTER 2

# Human Nature

*'The only way to make sense out of change is to plunge into it, move with it, and join the dance. No valid plans for the future can be made by those who have no capacity for living now. I have realised that the past and future are real illusions, that they exist in the present, which is what there is and all there is'.*

Alan Watts

I find it interesting that the more we learn and the more realisations we come to in life, the more we want to change others. Basically we take the knowledge, understand it thoroughly, but then we go on a mission to transform others – all the while tending to think we know it all. Many times, we do this unconsciously, but this way is not very clever. We need to start with ourselves, to transcend ourselves first before we worry about others. In addition to that, it is not our job to go on a mission to try to change others, growth may happen but it cannot be forced, it shall happen naturally in its own time.

The Buddha did not leave the palace and start preaching to people; he went through the entire process of enlightenment and understanding, and only after he felt enlightened did he start to preach. He was already a living example of what he would preach about. I am not suggesting, however, that in order to teach and share ideas we need to be living the path: the message is far more important than the messenger.

The philosopher Alan Watts is a living example of the point I am trying to make. He focused on bringing Eastern philosophy to the West. He also focused on the teachings of Zen Buddhism and Taoism among other things. Yet he said he was not a Zen Buddhist nor advocated it, he was simply sharing a point of view that he enjoyed. Alan Watts was one of the greatest philosophers of all time, who gave us insight into areas such as death by helping us fully understand the concept of nature and our nature as part of the vast amazing universe, how to fully enjoy the present moment, removing anxiety, understanding love, impermanence, attachment and religions to mention a few. By listening to his thought-provoking teachings or reading his books, one may easily come to the conclusion that he was enlightened – as his teachings lead to enlightenment if you truly make the effort to follow them.

Nonetheless, many people are shocked to learn that he was a serious alcoholic who normally gave his seminars while under the influence. When his daughter Anne asked him about his excessive alcohol consumption, he said, 'I like myself more when I am drunk', but did not elaborate further. He was an ordinary man, who married three times and had seven children, but was never a present father, and there are rumours that he had cheated in his relationships. Based on the nature of his teachings you wouldn't expect him to live that lifestyle. This is to say, what is of greater importance is the message and not the messenger. Unfortunately, people tend to place more focus on the persona and want to idealise others; they may feel very disappointed and even cheated once they find out that their teacher is indeed a normal human being. I have witnessed many accounts of people who basically stopped benefiting from Watts's teachings simply because they found out that he was an alcoholic.

Alan Watts used to call himself a philosophical entertainer, the entertainer of ideas, and as far as I understand, he didn't really want any followers. When he went to Japan and spent time learning Zen Buddhism, he was very disappointed to find out that the monks were normal people just like us with all the imperfections of humans. They weren't angels or pure people. With time he came to the realisation that they had already gone through the process of trying to fight their nature as humans, and that the state of awakeness was indeed when we become aware of our nature as fallible human beings, learn to accept our flaws, and simply surrender as there is absolutely nothing else we can do. We must finally realise that the whole idea of self-improvement is a hoax. Another interesting aspect of self-improvement is that the person who tries to improve is the one who needs to be improved; there, immediately, we have a vicious circle. If we wish to improve ourselves, we shall do it through a higher source. This source could be God, or, for those who don't believe in the conventional definition of God, they can connect with their higher self, the atman, 'the real self ', which is essentially identical with God. We have our lower self, which we call the ego, and trying to seek self-improvement through it ends in a vicious circle.

Going back to what I said previously, it is basically impossible to achieve perfection due to our nature as human beings, and therefore it is not realistic to set expectations for the one who conveys the message. In fact, how do we know what is good for other people? How do we know what is good for us? If we say that we want to improve, we ought to know what is good for us, but obviously we don't–otherwise we would be improved.

If we do agree that being enlightened is related to understanding our nature as fallible human beings, stop trying to control things to conform to our will, stop trying to force things, stop being self-defensive, and basically surrendering to the idea that there is nothing we can do to be better, could it be that even though Alan Watts was an alcoholic he could still be enlightened? That maybe he drank because he simply enjoyed it and not as a form of escape? Are there any rules with regards to being enlightened, or guidelines for it? Who are we to say who is enlightened and who is not?

# CHAPTER 3

## Work as Play

*'The meaning of life is just to be alive. It is so plain and so obvious and so simple. And yet, everybody rushes around in a great panic as if it were necessary to achieve something beyond themselves'.*

Alan Watts

When I was still working in the corporate environment, I sat down with the CEO and he asked me, *'What job would you have if money were no object?'*

I don't remember what I answered at the stage, probably that I would have liked to work in the psychology field. But that question reminded me of an inspiring YouTube video I once heard on the subject, and when I got home I listened to it again and the message touched me deeply. That was my first conscious exposure to Alan Watts– and as they say, 'when the student is ready, the teacher appears'. From that moment I started listening to more and more of his teachings. Today I still listen every day to the audios I've probably heard more than fifty times by now. Some people would criticise the fact that I tend to disregard other philosophers or teachings and only focus on one perspective. However, my whole life I have been listening to different perspectives. I was involved in different roles at the company doing multiple things, and, as the years went by, I realised that I had some knowledge of and could do all sort of things but I did not master anything. I couldn't confidently say that I was brilliant at something.

With regards to Alan Watts, his philosophical perspective resonated with me. I had finally found my ground, something I wanted to be with and master, and I have to say it was the best thing I ever did. When I went to London to specialise in cognitive behavioural therapy (CBT) and hypnotherapy as well as rational emotive behavioural therapy (REBT) I did the exact same thing – I immersed myself in something that resonated with me. Since then I have focused on the specific teachings of specific psychologists (which also has its criticism), but today I can see the benefits of my path because I am really good at what I do. I mastered it, I love it, and I am closer to becoming an expert in my field.

When I left my job as communications manager, most people told me my decision was unwise. They said I should keep my job and do it part-time until I had enough income as a therapist to leave the comfort and stability of my job. But that wouldn't have allowed me to succeed in my career as a therapist. I wouldn't have had enough time or energy to do anything well because I would be drained from work. And at that stage I knew what I wanted and there was no turning back. I knew that regardless of how difficult the path, I would do my best and hope for the best.

I am sharing this with you because when you ask most people about what they are passionate about, or what they would do if money were no object, they come up with all sort of things such as design, painting, being an actor, or being a writer. But they often say that they couldn't make a living from it or get rich, so they choose a profession that guarantees financially stability or wealth. So what happens? They choose a career path for the wrong reasons, and they get no satisfaction from life because our career occupies most of our time in life. They end up not being great at what they do because they have no drive, no love for their work, and their job is basically perceived as a stressful chore. Then they come up with memes on social media about hating Mondays and being overly excited about Fridays. They are living for the weekends and holidays.

I could no longer live like that. I knew that life didn't have to be that way and surely there was another path upon which I would no longer hate Mondays. If you are passionate about something, you will be with it – you will effortlessly place all of your energy into it and, by doing that, you become an expert in it. And don't worry too much because anything you are interested in, you will find someone else also interested in it.

Many people also told me I couldn't be successful as a therapist in Mozambique because people don't have the custom of going to therapists, nor do they understand the importance of therapy. I did it anyway, and I will tell you I am happy. I no longer hate Mondays, I love what I do, and very early in my career I started making more than

enough for the month. I have been able to bring awareness to people about my philosophy, and 95 per cent of the clients who have come to me, come through referrals from existing clients or people who understand what I do. This means that I don't really need to do my own marketing, my clients do it for me because of the excellence they see in my work. Why do they see that? Because I do what I do naturally, and it is very difficult to perceive it as work when I am doing what I truly love. I literally found out a way to get paid for playing.

David Orr, the ecologist and writer, once said, *'The planet does not need more "successful" people. But it does desperately need more peacemakers, healers, restorers, storytellers, and lovers of every kind. It needs people who you have no fear of living with side by side. It needs people who live well in their places. In needs people of moral courage willing to join the fight to make the world habitable and humane. And these qualities have little to do with "success" as we have defined it.'* I can tell you that you don't chase success, success comes naturally as a result of your great work – and the only way to do great work is to love what you do. People often

*Sharlene Sema Raston*

ask me when the best time is to take action and I normally answer: NOW.

If we continue to wait until the right time to do things, we will never get there. We will come up with countless excuses to postpone things because it's basically impossible to find the perfect time when all conditions align to take action. If that's what you're looking for, most likely you'll never act. The excuses we normally make are due to the fear of the unknown and not wanting to deal with the discomfort of leaving our comfort zone. Keep in mind that great things usually happen when we are outside our comfort zone.

*'This is the real secret of life – to be completely engaged with what you are doing in the here and now. And instead of calling it "work," realise that it is play'.*

Alan Watts

# CHAPTER 4

# Social Media

Social media is a platform where we can choose our reputations, and some people prefer to look stupid indeed. My advice to you is to stop sharing your happiness on social media, simply stop. Most people do not enjoy or want to see others doing a lot better than they are – this can bring out envy and negativity. On social media, people try their best to portray their lives as being amazing, mainly on Facebook and Instagram – which is fake. We see couples showing ultimate love and compassion, accompanied by sweet dedications, yet weeks later we hear they are separated because their relationship has been terrible over the past months. If that is the case, why fake it on social media? To make people envious and jealous? To deceive people into thinking their lives are awesome and they are the happiest couple on earth?

I'm not fully sure, but I perceive it as ridiculous. The mask we wear on social media and the messages we try to get across, the memes we post to give the impression

that we are enlightened – these are nothing more than an act. Funny enough, most people buy the lie and become depressed or sad as they start to believe that the grass really is greener on the other side.

Most people on social media tend to portray themselves as having a happy and perfect life. But in reality, each selfie posted is probably the result of taking ten photos and selecting the best one, followed by a filtering process, and then: 'Hurray!!! We look stunning'. The accuracy of the photo is non-existent. People tend to post about trips and wealth, which may make others not only feel envious but depressed; lower self-esteem is basically inevitable in the comparison.

When we speak about addictions, we are no longer only referring to alcohol, drugs, and gambling. The greatest of all addictions is social media. When someone posts a photo, with the unconscious aim of getting dopamine release, they continuously monitor the likes and comments. As the number of reactions increases, dopamine is released in the social media user's brain. The opposite also applies: if the amount of comments and likes does not meet our expectations, we tend to feel miserable, and this may automatically affect our self-esteem.

Dopamine is the chemical in our brain that is responsible for happiness, which means that every time we have positive experiences and feel happy, dopamine is released in the brain. For every time we get a like or nice comments, dopamine is released. This is the very same chemical that is released when someone does drugs, drinks alcohol, eats chocolate, or is in love, to mention a few.

In this new era, we have lost all patience to wait and fight for things because we are more inclined towards instant gratification and quick results. Instead of going out and naturally meeting people, we may prefer to use Tinder. Then we don't need to feel shy while trying to win over someone, and we don't practice social skills. We no longer have time to eat at a restaurant or buy and cook food; we prefer drive-throughs. These methods contribute to having things instantly, but they do not lead to life satisfaction, job satisfaction, or strengthening our relationships. Unfortunately there are no apps for those things.

If we plan to be happier, we shall understand that relationships take time and effort to build and that, in order to have job satisfaction, we also need a skill set and understanding. Even though the journey takes time and patience, it tends to be more real and deeper if done in the natural manner of human interaction.

# CHAPTER 5

# Mental Masturbation

Mental masturbation is the art of overwhelming ourselves with inspirational quotes, self-development books, and motivational speeches without ever putting them into practice. It is the art of watching other people's wins, their achievements, their tips for living on a regular basis, but not taking action in our own lives. Knowledge that is not applied is a total waste and basically not productive at all. Great things start happening outside of our comfort zone, and these things only happen when we take action–then we can see significant changes. As an example, within CBT, it is crucial that people put into practice what they have learnt because theory alone will never be enough to promote change. Just as when we get our driving license, first we learn the theory. Even when we have mastered the theoretical material successfully, we can't get in the car and start driving. When we actually start learning how to drive, we may find it difficult at first and feel anxious on the road. But the more we practice, the less anxious we feel and the better we drive. Eventually the driving process becomes fully automatic. This is to illustrate the importance of practice and of applying what we have learnt.

I have found that many clients engaged in other forms of therapy tend to complain that even though they understand something in theory, it is a challenge to incorporate the teachings into their everyday lives. This may be because these therapies simply don't offer the skills and techniques to actually apply the theory into their everyday lives. This is one of the main reasons why I love the CBT's perspective.

Mental masturbation can be compared to someone who simply sits at home and starts imagining all the awesome and different scenarios of being with his crush without taking any action to win the girl over. You can watch 1,000 self-improvement videos, but none of it will amount to anything if you won't act. Misery is comfortable, whereas working towards our goals takes effort but definitely is worth the shot. So, this is what you need to do: replace daydreaming and excessive theorising with taking action and be aware that the world will not give you love, happiness, or anything else for being a nice person – you have to reach out and take it for yourself.

On a completely different note, I have also found that people with the mentality of 'I must be who I am, and people shall love me for who I am' don't seem to have thought this idea through. First of all, we are in constant change. Who we were yesterday is not the same person as who we are today or will be tomorrow. Nothing is set in stone. In addition, I am not very sure who this 'I' is, and I think many people share my confusion, because when I ask them they usually struggle to answer. If they do start describing their 'I', they most likely refer to the constructs they were born with, indoctrinated into, or that highly influenced them in the environment in which they lived. It could be something like pride in their race, religion (into which they were indoctrinated), or lack of religion (also indoctrinated); their perspectives on life, which have been directly influenced by their environment; the nature of their exposure to external events; their values, which are often related to the type of education they had; the country they live in; their conditions and what they have learnt from their parents and significant others; as well as their life experiences.

So, who is this 'I' that people love to go on and on about? The ego is a fabrication, which some people spend the rest of their lives standing up for, without realising that the ego is not as special or authentic as they make it out be. Have you realised that we, just like any other living being, are seen equally by nature? Nature is reckless when it decides to have an earthquake, tsunami, or other catastrophe. Nature does not perceive us as special individuals who should be protected, but as a whole, just like any other living being. I might even say that nature is more concerned about species as opposed to individuals. It is time to wake up now and find out who we really are – our real selves are not victims of fate or puppets that life pushes around. The real, deep down self is the whole universe.

In relation to finding a mate or succeeding in the corporate world, if that is the case, we need to stop the rubbish of thinking that 'people must love me for who I am'. There are over seven billion people on this earth, thousands of whom share the same personality or even the same look as you. If the plan is to succeed, we shall realise that we are part of a system that has rules. If we are to be part of it, we shall go with the flow too, swimming with and not against the river. We shall come to the conclusion and understanding that life is a game and that we should fully perceive it as play. Do you think you are special? You are not; acknowledge reality, put in the work, and play to win.

# CHAPTER 6

# Rational Emotive Behavioural Therapy in a Nutshell

When I decided to fully follow my passion and went to London for training in psychotherapy, CBT was the field that most resonated with me. I was extremely happy to finally find a psychological perspective that fully aligned with my beliefs.

I perceive CBT as psychoeducation in many aspects because we teach the clients many techniques from how to undisturb themselves, to identifying the reasons why they become disturbed, to coping mechanisms, philosophy, and so on. What follows is a brief overview of CBT, as I fully believe that you will benefit from it, too.

Albert Ellis had been working for many years in psychoanalysis and found it unhelpful as clients would take too much time in the therapy process and the results were very poor. He once stated that, 'Freud has a gene for inefficiency, and I think I have a gene for efficiency'. Ellis decided to start his own therapy approach, which he called Rational Emotive Behavioural Therapy (REBT). This is a philosophical perspective within the CBT approach that aims to help clients change their philosophy on life. Ellis encouraged the therapist and clients to perceive REBT as a philosophy of life.

The basic notion of REBT is that the events in our lives do not disturb us, but rather it is our philosophy and perspective of those events that leads to emotional disturbance. We disturb ourselves, and therefore, if we have the capacity to disturb ourselves, we have an equal capacity to undisturb ourselves.

What I love about REBT is that it focuses fully on the present moment. We believe that the past partially contributes to our emotional disturbance, but the past is not responsible for it – our philosophy and perspectives play the main role in our emotional disturbance. Therefore, we don't spend much time dwelling on the past, trying to find the causes of the problem; we are more interested in what is maintaining the condition and not allowing the client to move on. In other words, we consider 'why' an ineffective question and are more interest in 'what' happens instead.

I have always been very frustrated with the fact that therapists have too many rules to regulate their own behaviour, which include not being able to self-disclose, not being direct, and not expressing opinions. When I encountered REBT I was delighted to find that Ellis also hated this aspect and that is why he started a new form of therapy. On the other hand, in REBT, the client does not lead the therapy as in many other forms of therapy. Here the therapist leads the session, he or she is seen as the expert in the field, and Ellis suggested that a therapist may be perceived as a teacher. I also love that REBT allows therapists' self-disclosure because we believe that it can strengthen the connection with the therapist, and helps the client feel as if the therapist can relate. Our main goal is to teach clients all the necessary skills and provide them with the tools that will allow them to become their own therapists and no longer depend on an external therapist.

Albert Ellis identified some of the beliefs that lead to emotional disturbance such as:

- Everybody must love us and treat us well, otherwise they deserve to burn in hell.

- Everything must happen the way we want and when we want, otherwise it is the end of the world.

- One shall be competent, adequate, and succeed in everything, otherwise one is no good.

He found that:

1. **Demands** normally lead to emotional disturbance such as 'musts' and 'shoulds'. One example is 'People must love me and approve me'. These demands are normally rigid and

inflexible; demands shall be replaced by preferences instead, which are more flexible, realistic, and less rigid.

**Awfulising** is when we make an unrealistic assessment of badness or perceive negative events as 'end of the world bad'. For example, by saying, 'It will be awful if I don't reach my sales target this month', we exaggerate our perspective of things and we see certain situations as 100 per cent bad or awful.

1. **Low frustration tolerance**, which is the belief that one cannot bear it if one's demands are not met. Then we show an inability to tolerate frustration. We normally use terms such as 'I cannot stand it' or 'it is unbearable'.

2. **Damming of self**, world, and others. We do this when we tend to globally and negatively rate oneself, others, or the world based on one trait. For example, an individual who does not reach the sales target for the month may rate him-or herself as a failure, which is not a realistic perspective.

These beliefs are perceived as irrational because they generate emotional disturbance or unhealthy negative emotions; therefore, our goal is to change these unhealthy beliefs into healthier versions, which are more realistic, flexible, and logical. Rational beliefs are based on wants, preferences, and desires, and because they are logical and realistic, they do not lead to emotional disturbance—they help the individual toward achieving his or her goals and to experience healthy negative emotions as opposed to unhealthy negative emotions. For example, instead of feeling anxiety or depression, the individual would rather feel concerned or sad.

Note that we are not positivists; we are realists. Therefore, if a very strong negative event happens in your life, you will undoubtedly feel a negative emotion. But there are healthy negative emotions and unhealthy negative emotions. The healthy negative emotions are viewed as a natural response to negative events that helps the individual behave in a constructive way, accept what cannot be changed, and be realistic. Examples of healthy negative emotions are concern, sadness, healthy anger or annoyance, remorse, regret, disappointment, healthy jealousy, and healthy envy. On the other hand, unhealthy negative emotions are unrealistic, leading to emotional disturbance and making us behave in an unproductive and non-constructive manner. Some examples are anxiety, depression, anger, guilt, shame, hurt, jealousy, and envy.

If we find that our clients have a healthy emotional response to negative events, they can be dismissed, as they do not need therapy, but to strengthen their emotional support through friends and family, for instance.

## Chapter 7

## The Model of Emotional Disturbance

Today I can firmly state that happiness is not something that you chase, it is not a place that you can travel to and conquer, and it is not at the end of a line you will reach at a certain point in your life – it is exactly where you are. Happiness is a state of mind you choose. If you struggle to achieve it, I can easily conclude that this is the result of your being a slave to the mind instead of the master. We allow our minds to poison us with all sorts of distorted and irrational thinking, which is accompanied by unhealthy negative emotions. In contrast, being the master of our mind allows us to be fully aware of our thoughts and how they influence our feelings and behaviour. By understanding our minds, we can challenge any unhealthy and unrealistic thoughts and replace them with realistic, flexible, and healthy thoughts. If this exercise is done repetitively on a regular basis, we will have these thoughts automatically or unconsciously, which shall allow us to live a happier and fulfilled life. In rational emotive behavioural therapy, we use a template called the ABCDE model of emotional disturbance.

The ABCDE model was created by Albert Ellis and Windy Dryden. 'A' refers to Activating Event, which is the event that triggers an emotional disturbance. 'B' refers to one's irrational Belief about the event A. And 'C' is the Emotional and Behavioural Consequences. Most people are under the impression that A leads to C. For example, someone may say that he is angry because his partner went out without telling him. This is an example of the A–C conclusion. In REBT, however, we believe that it is not A that causes C, but B that causes C, where B is the belief someone holds in relation to A. For instance, if the partner interprets the lack of communication as a direct sign of not caring, of being reckless and disrespectful, the person shall experience unhealthy negative emotions such as jealously or anger. This is an example of an irrational and unrealistic thinking, only because there is absolutely no evidence that she was trying to be reckless or disrespectful. On the other hand, if the partner perceives the behaviour as unpleasant but does not jump to any rigid conclusions, the partner shall experience healthy negative emotions. In this case, the partner would experience annoyance and concern for his relationship. We shall experience healthy negative emotions when our interpretation of the event is realistic and flexible, and this leads to healthy emotions and behaviours that are more constructive and productive. Instead of shouting and being upset with his partner, he could then be assertive instead and show empathy by trying to understand the situation.

Once we identify all of the unhealthy negative beliefs we go to 'D', which stands for **Disputes** or arguments against irrational beliefs. At this stage we ask questions such as:

a) Is it logical to think that because your partner did not inform you that she was going out, it automatically means that she does not care about you?

b) Is there any evidence that proves that because she did not inform you, it definitely means that she does not care?

c) How helpful is it to you to hold those beliefs?

Lastly, the 'E' stands for **establishing new beliefs**, which replace the irrational, unrealistic, and rigid beliefs with rational, flexible, and realistic beliefs in relation to the event. An example would be, 'I don't enjoy it when my partner goes out without letting me know; it is unpleasant but it is not the end of the world. I shall discuss it with her by making sure she understands why it is important for me that she keeps me informed and in order to reduce the probability of it happening again'.

By using the ABCDE model of emotional disturbance, we can safely conclude that we are not puppets of fate and that we can have control over our unhealthy negative emotions by replacing them with healthier versions.

## Chapter 8

## The Sociopath World

*'Of course everything comes at a price-we wouldn't be doing it if we weren't getting something from you, often money or power or simply even the enjoyment of your admiration and desire'.*

−M.E. Thomas, Confessions of a Sociopath: A Life Spent Hiding in Plain Sight.

When we hear the term 'sociopath', most people tend to imagine a serial killer, a violent individual, or someone who looks like a criminal and has had many encounters with the legal system for transgressing the law. However, you would be surprised to know that recent research shows that one out of twenty-five people are sociopaths, and they are much harder to spot than you would imagine. Research shows that most sociopaths are found in higher positions in the corporate world; in fact, the chosen position for a sociopath is that of CEO. They don't usually achieve the position through merit, but due to their Machiavellic nature that believes that the end justifies the means, their strong ability to manipulate people to achieve what they want, and their strong desire for winning, power, and money.

Welcome to the sociopath's world–a world full of charm, confidence, manipulation, compulsive lying, no empathy, the strong desire for winning, power, cost-benefit analysis, and pure grandiosity. I have always been fascinated by sociopaths because their persona is most probably the most difficult to understand. In fact there is no cure for sociopathy, so if you find that your partner is a sociopath, you can be assured that he or she will remain a sociopath despite promises to change. Even if he or she manages to incorporate a changed persona for a little while, it never lasts, and, in no time, the sociopath will be back to his or her standard behaviour. Compulsive lying and manipulating people is a lot easier for sociopaths than being real, and just like an alcoholic will drink impulsively, the sociopath has a strong impulse to manipulate people and tell lies.

I am writing this chapter with the aim of bringing awareness to people to help them identify sociopaths and reduce their chances of being manipulated by or a victim of one. These personas are so well acted that the individual can basically become anything he or she wishes with such confidence that it would never cross your mind that the persona you are dealing with is basically a fake identity. They are very intelligent individuals, creative, their confidence levels are very high, and they believe in their own lies; it is therefore very easy to become a victim of one. Unfortunately, it does not take very long until their mask falls off and people start to realise that they are in fact con artists, which makes it very difficult for sociopaths to maintain their relationships and jobs.

Okay, at this point you may have thought of someone you think is a sociopath, or indeed you might have thought of yourself. Before we jump to strong conclusions, let's take a look at the different characteristics to look out for.

1. **They lack conscience or empathy.**

Sociopaths are not very good at putting themselves in someone else's shoes or feeling sympathy for others. They normally lack on emotions such as guilt, remorse, sympathy, or pity. Whereas most people would say, 'think before you act', their motto is 'act first and think later'. This means that they are highly impulsive and tend to respond to their emotions without putting much thought into the consequences of their actions. This may be very dangerous if the person has violent tendencies as it may lead to violent behaviour if any strong negative emotion is triggered. However, regardless of their actions they do not feel remorse for their actions and they tend to be very cold-hearted.

A sociopath once told me:

'Many times, I think that I do not have emotions.'

When discussing murderers, he told me that he truly believes that everyone's destiny has been premeditated, and therefore if he ever killed someone it would mean that it was in that person's fate to die that day. Since he would simply be the instrument to fulfil what was already written, there was no need to feel guilty about it.

2. **They lack emotions in response to events, and their capacity to love is very limited.**

When they do appear to be in love and act accordingly it is normally as a means to achieve what they want. They can become the most loving creature on earth and the best lover you can ever have; they study your behaviour in detail and listen to your weaknesses, your needs, and what you are looking for – and they become it exactly. The act is so convincing that you start to believe you have found your soulmate.

He will tell you that he loves you very early in the relationship, how he has waited for you his whole life, and isn't it amazing that the two of you are exactly the same, love the same things, and complement each other? On top of that, you have met each other at the perfect time in your lives, which reinforces the idea that you are meant for each other and always have been. You would never imagine that you are in fact dealing with a con artist. 'Con artist' stands for confidence artist, and their high success rate in the manipulation of others through the different tools they use is mainly due to their high confidence levels.

I once asked a sociopath if he ever suffered from any breakup in his life and his response was:

*'No, I have never suffered from leaving any of my relationships, not sure why? Probably because I was the one messing things up'.*

3. **Sociopaths are very attentive and they love to lure their victims when they can sense vulnerability.**

One of the sociopath's most important features is the need to gain control, and if she has met you and comes to the realisation that you have what she wants, you may become a victim of **love bombing**. With this technique, the sociopath flatters and overwhelms you with constant texts, phone calls, emails, and social media comments, or by spending excessive time with you. At first you may feel as if she has placed you on a pedestal; she literally makes you believe that in such a short period of time she has fallen totally in love with you. Everything may feel like a dream or a movie that later on you realise was indeed fiction.

Dating a sociopath feels like eating a very delicious cake without realising there is poison inside, whereas dating a normal person feels like eating a piece of fruit. It is not amazing; however, it is real, constant, and follows the natural process of a healthy relationship, which takes time to build.

So she already assessed you, she knows exactly what you want to hear, she starts mirroring you and gaining full control over you through the excessive communication. You may find that the relationship starts interfering with your other activities, with the other relationships you have, and all of a sudden you find that she is gaining your full attention to focus on her only.

In a recent case involving a relationship with a sociopath, the sociopath told his partner that he tended to suffer from severe panic attacks that were mostly predominant when he was alone as he couldn't be alone with his own mind. Negative thoughts would come to his mind, and he literally felt that he might go crazy and start panicking. As a result, every time she had to go somewhere, the sociopath would immediately start experiencing the symptoms of the panic attacks, and so she would do everything in a rush to stay with him and calm him down. While she was away, the shower of messages were non-stop—too much love and attention, which literally gave her no time to focus on anything other than him.

*Why love bombing?*

Through love bombing, the sociopath does not give the partner time to think about the situation or spend with others; it isolates the partner and intensifies the relationship in a short period by making it move extremely quickly.

### 4. They are narcissistic and have a grandiose self-image and superficial charm.

Sociopaths think they are superior to others; they feel strong admiration for themselves, their looks, and their immense charm. In fact, they use the charm to manipulate their victims and mimic the emotions of others. To show emotion, they try to look as if they are crying, and, if they are lucky, they manage to get two tears down their face.

### 5. They are sensitive to criticism.

You may notice that sociopaths dislike any form of criticism. They will easily play the victim even if it involves lying in the process because they are constantly looking for approval from others. They would literally prefer to run away from a problem, changing topics or becoming aggressive as opposed to listening to criticism.

You will notice that once their mask falls away and you are fully aware of their lies, once you try to confront them, they will shower you with even more lies. They will find ways to blame other people or you for their behaviour to make you believe that their behaviour was conditioned and justified. They will minimise the severity of the problem to zero and find all the tactics and ways possible to escape from it. They may also escape by moving away from you and find another vulnerable victim who will feed their ego instead.

Remember that it is all about them – all about their ego and making them feel superior and special.

## 6. They exercise poor judgment and have an inability to learn from experience.

Earlier on this chapter, I mentioned that there is basically no cure for sociopaths. Yes, no cure. This means that they will continue making the same mistakes and maintaining the same behaviour regardless of how many times their mask falls off. They will move on to the next target and implement the exact same tactics they used on the previous targets. They lack remorse and shame; they have

an unreliable nature, lack of insight, and general poverty in major affective reactions; and they fail to follow through on any life plan.

## 7. Their inability to understand emotions and lack of trust in people make them very vulnerable to paranoia and excessive control.

In a relationship with a sociopath, you will notice that they want full control of your behaviour by constantly checking on you. They may become paranoid over small things: if you are on the phone for a while, and they are trying to contact you, they might quickly jump to suspicious conclusions. This paranoia combined with their impulsive nature may mean they will easily snap at you. Once you finish your call, you may find an angry message from them suspecting that you were cheating on them over the phone, for example.

Compulsive lying is part of their second nature as it is part of their philosophy that the means justify the end. If confronted with lies, they will easily justify their lies with more lies, and, in the process, they will find a way to play the victim. You might just find yourself apologising to them without realising that the game has been reversed and all of a sudden you are in the wrong.

## 8. They exhibit promiscuous behaviour.

You will find that most sociopaths tend to get involved in numerous relationships. They are capable of maintaining several relationships at the same time, do not discriminate between partners, and can easily move from one relationship to another without going through the expected sadness and suffering that an average person would experience.

A sociopath once shared with me that he opened a broadcast list on WhatsApp with plenty of women and every morning he would send a good morning message, or another sweet message based on the occasion, to all of them at the same time. This made each woman feel special, believing that he actively thought of her in the morning and sent her a cute message. But the reality was that she was simply one of many. Sociopaths will use their tactics everywhere and continue to lure people until one of them softens up and may well become the next victim.

Due to the fact that sociopaths lack feelings of shame, it makes it easier for them to literally try every single woman because they do not fear rejection or taking risks, and seducing many women simultaneously increases their chances of scoring in comparison to a non-sociopath.

### 9. They are irresponsible.

Sociopaths tend toward a parasitic lifestyle, and you may easily find yourself supporting them financially and in other aspects. They may manage to manipulate you to the extent that they become the core and centre of your life. You may find yourself living to fulfil their needs without realising you slack in all other aspects of your life. You will notice that they lack the ability to honour their commitments, that they are unreliable in many ways, and that they tend to not respect the boundaries imposed by others and focus only on their self-needs.

As I mentioned above, when you meet them, they may tell you about their achievements, work history, and current employment, and with time you may come to the realisation that it was all fictitious and that their past and present moment is a lot less interesting than what they portrayed.

### 10. They have a history of juvenile delinquency.

Even though sociopaths are not necessarily aggressive, you are likely to find that in their teens they have a history of aggression, antagonism, ruthlessness, tough-mindedness, and manipulation. They may share stories about fights they have been involved in which may be shared in a distorted manner, or you may notice certain scars or abnormalities on their bodies without being given a clear explanation.

The points above are some of the main features you can look for to determine whether you are dating a sociopath or how to spot one. These are overall characteristics, and a full diagnosis by a psychiatrist based on the Diagnostic and Statistical Manual of Mental Disorders needs to be done to fully confirm the diagnosis.

If you do realise that you have been a victim of a sociopath's tactics and love bombing, you may feel guilt and shame. However, you have simply been a victim among many others of a creative, intelligent, and manipulative confidence artist. Everything was premeditated, and the sociopath made sure to lure you in when you were at your most vulnerable. They are so good at what they do that they can make you believe you are living a dream. They prey on very intelligent people, who some claim are easier to manipulate. The most important thing at the moment is that you are now aware and you can take measures to free yourself, overcome the toxic relationship, and move on to live a happier life.

# Chapter 9

# The Story about the Fisherman

*(A well-known story I once heard)*

There was once a businessman who was sitting by the beach in a small Brazilian village.

As he sat, he saw a Brazilian fisherman rowing a small boat towards the shore having caught quite few big fish. The businessman was impressed and asked the fisherman, *'How long does it take you to catch so many fish?'*

The fisherman replied, *'Oh, just a short while'.*

*'Then why don't you stay longer at sea and catch even more?'*

The businessman was astonished.

*'This is enough to feed my whole family',* the fisherman said.

The businessman then asked, *'So, what do you do for the rest of the day?'*

The fisherman replied, *'Well, I usually wake up early in the morning, go out to sea and catch a few fish, then go back and play with my kids. In the afternoon, I take a nap with my wife, and evening comes, I join my buddies in the village for a drink – we play guitar, sing and dance throughout the night'.*

The businessman offered a suggestion to the fisherman:

I have a PhD in business management. I could help you to become a more successful person. From now on, you should spend more time at sea and try to catch as many fish as possible. When you have saved enough money, you could buy a bigger boat and catch even more fish. Soon you will be able to afford to buy more boats, set up your own company, your own production plant for canned food and distribution network. By then, you will have moved out of this village and to São Paulo, where you can set up HQ to manage your other branches.

The fisherman continued, *'And after that?'*

The businessman laughed heartily, *'After that, you can live like a king in your own house, and when the time is right, you can go public and float your shares on the stock exchange, and you will be rich'.*

The fisherman asked, *'And after that?'*

The businessman said, *'After that, you can finally retire, you can move to a house by the fishing village, wake up early in the morning, catch a few fish, then return home to play with kids, have a nice afternoon nap with your wife, and when evening comes, you can join your buddies for a drink, play the guitar, sing and dance throughout the night!'*

The fisherman was puzzled. *'Isn't that what I am doing now?'*

*Sharlene Sema Raston*

## Chapter 10

## The Beauty of Silence

Most times when I am sitting next to someone, I feel obliged to make conversation even if it's going to be rubbish, such as speaking about the weather. We have been made to believe that silence between two people is negative, and this belief leads to feelings of discomfort if we are to simply be silent. I have finally come to the realisation that speaking all the time is not necessary and I have also learnt to appreciate silence. It is okay to stay silent!

At Kopan Monastery, where I attended the ten-day retreat course, Discovering Buddhism, one of the rules was that we had to keep silent every day from 9:00 p.m. until 2:00 p.m., which meant that the only meal we could actually enjoy conversing together at was dinner. The last three days of the retreat, we had to stay in complete silence. Every now and then I would try to make a sound or say a word just to check that my voice was still there.

I still remember when our teacher told us that she sometimes overheard our conversations and judged them as meaningless – that we conversed just for the sake of speaking, asking questions like, 'Where are you from?' She somehow knew that we didn't really care about the answer, but at that moment we were asking for the sake of speaking, to break the silence.

The whole idea of engaging with silence was to help us focus on the teachings, but it had other advantages, too: it allowed us to fully contemplate the beautiful view during our meals, focus on the taste of the delicious food, and taught us that speaking for the sake of speaking was not necessary. When we speak, we are repeating information that we already know. When we listen, we have the opportunity to learn something new.

Most people are scared of silence, or are constantly trying to keep themselves busy so as not to sit alone with their thoughts – why is that? Why is it that people are constantly trying to escape from themselves and are scared to observe their minds and the thoughts that come and go without judgement? Why is it that people don't want to let go of commanding their thoughts and become watchers?

I am by no means saying that we should always remain silent as I am extremely talkative. But if you have nothing to say, it is better to keep quiet and not force conversation. Remember to speak only when you feel that your words are better than the silence.

*Sharlene Sema Raston*

# CHAPTER 11

# Kopan Monastery Experience

Many people have asked me, 'Why Nepal? What is it like to stay at a Tibetan monastery?' I found my little diary where I wrote down a few ideas that were going through my mind as I left the monastery and returned to my home country–Mozambique. Today I have decided to share the diary with you.

Kopan Monastery, situated on a hill in Kathmandu, teaches the Gelug tradition of Tibetan Mahayana Buddhism and was founded by two great masters, Lama Yeshe (1935–1984) and Lama Zopa Rinpoche (b.1945). At Kopan I had the most amazing experience, which no words can do justice to. It wasn't about reading and trying to understand the teachings. It was about feeling what I had learnt without the necessity of words.

*I am on the plane, and it breaks my heart to leave such a precious place. It is so painful to leave all the peace I have felt for two weeks and go back to the real world.*

*The world where compassion is lacking – the materialistic world where everything is superficial and about escaping, where ignorance prevails. Money is perceived as the most important factor and goal to most people, which results in an attachment to the material world based on the belief that the material world can eventually fulfil us. This way of thinking is tricky because the more we have, the more we want; it's a never-ending cycle.*

*So the interesting question is: how much money or material possessions is enough? When can someone actually say, 'I have got enough wealth and I am finally happy?' I have never heard that before, because we've never understood that the hole we are trying to fill in the quest for happiness can never be filled with material things. We all have something in common – we want to be happy! The wisdom lies in looking for happiness in the right direction. Unfortunately, we haven't deeply understood that attachment to the material world is one of the main causes of our suffering.*

*When we are young, we think that if we have all the chocolate in the world, we will be happy. Once we get older we think that if we have a good partner next to us, a good job, a nice car, and money, that we will be happy. Unfortunately even having those wishes and ideas fulfilled, we still struggle to feel happy. The question is: where does the problem lie?*

*Sharlene Sema Raston*

*We try to reach happiness with things that can only bring us temporary happiness. Ignorance leads to attachment, attachment leads to anger, and anger leads to suffering.*

*We need learn to pursue everlasting happiness, which can be achieved by cultivating compassion towards all sentient beings, kindness, patience, freedom from attachment, and wisdom. By making others happy, we automatically become happy; the definition of compassion is not love only: compassion is the responsibility to help end the suffering of other sentient beings and to help others. Attachment can also lead to jealously, and jealously in turn leads to anger. Anger is the biggest obstacle to our happiness.*

*We need to learn to cultivate inner happiness by applying wisdom to our daily lives and by learning that there is no objective truth because it is all about perspective. We perceive things and events not the way they are, but by the way we are. There isn't anything more rewarding than being able to control one's emotions, feelings, anger, and how to react to a situation as awful as it may be. Our mind is like a two year old: we tell it not to do certain things, but the mind cannot follow our instructions because it has no discipline. As long as we are unable to control our thoughts, anger, and need for attachment, we will continue being slaves to our own thoughts and feelings; hence, the importance of meditating daily. Remember: Tame your mind.*

## Chapter 12

## Food for Thought

The realisation of the impermanence of life does not need to be perceived in a negative way; it is motivation to live to the fullest. The purpose of life is simply to live, and yet everyone is going around trying to achieve something. Life is a mystery; don't try to figure it out.

If the 'ego', which is what we tend to confuse as the 'I' or the 'self', were eternal, we would lose the drive to live fully. As we all know, human beings lose interest in things once they become permanent – hence the necessity to make life itself impermanent. The whole idea is to be fascinated with things, which is why, in the same way that people die, others are born so the universe can be perceived from the eyes of the child – with fascination.

We do belong somewhere. We belong to the universe and to nature, and the notion of death is an illusion. Death is simply part of the cycle of life in which we return to where we belong, the universe. We are all the 'I', but we can only experience it one at time. If we realise that there is no such thing as the 'self' because we can never know who we are, it becomes easier to detach from the ego – from the notion of and attachment to the self. Knowing ourselves is as impossible as knowing what our hug feels like.

We are all interconnected, and we learn about ourselves in relation to others and how other people experience us. Most people are not in with love their partner; they are in love with how the other person makes them feel. That is why once the other person stops giving them the desired feeling, they move on to the next person and may even develop feelings of resentment and anger towards their old partner. 'I love you, but only if you are with me'. Do you call that love or pure selfishness?

Our inner self is the divine which we tend to dismiss and act as if we were puppets of fate, slaves of what happens to us, as if everything were foreign; we forget karma. Karma means 'our own doing': everything that happens to us is our own doing. We are not always in control of our circumstances, but we are in control of how we react to them, our perceptions, and our attitudes and feelings. Let's become aware of our nature and remember that muddy water clears itself when left alone.

# Chapter 13

# Playing the Game of Life

I just want to find out: is it really very difficult to love another human being unconditionally even if he or she does not share the same perspective, religion, and way of doing things, culture, or even race for that matter?

When are we going to feel welcome – a sense of belonging even though we are different? Many people complain of being tired of not meeting others' expectations, of the conventional way of doing things, of the everyday routine and the hassle of the everyday life in order to achieve things that don't matter. Society, however, does not miss an opportunity to convince us that we do need things. I am speaking now about appearances, consumerism, capitalism, statuses – all the things that don't matter that people continue to chase every single day because they are told that these things are important. I confess, I once decided to abolish these things, and, to be honest, that didn't work either. If you want to be part of a society and be the odd one out, there is a probability that you may feel empty and frustrated, and therefore the other alternative is to play the game. The game is to put on an act, dress to impress – to say things that sound intelligent.

I have spoken about the concept of happiness before in which I made it clear that it is not a destination but a state of mind. Today I can think of a different definition, too, which is when there is congruence in what someone says and does. In other words, it is when I come to a point in which how I live aligns with what I believe in, and what I believe in aligns with what I say and do.

I believe the world we live in today is too superficial – we have become superficial and lost our essence. We do not know how to love our neighbour unconditionally; in fact, our judgements of people are based first on appearance. If, by any chance we do not like someone's appearance based on their looks, how they dress, or how they speak, we automatically don't give them a chance to show us who they really are. We also base our judgments on what we have heard about the person or past events that may no longer apply, predefining someone without enough knowledge of their person.

# CHAPTER 14

# What Do I Believe in?

I believe in the universe, I believe in mother nature—I believe in God and that we all have the divine within us. I believe that all religions are different mechanisms people use to get into contact with our higher self or with a higher power. That being said, I don't think there is only one correct religion and that all religions or paths are the right ones. Whatever path we choose is the right one and there is no one path/religion that fits all. In other words, people have the freedom to choose what path they relate to the most, which is normally based on their perspective of life, their culture, and their beliefs—all different perspectives are okay and shall be respected regardless.

I believe that for as much as we think that we are very special and have a serious purpose on this earth, we are not. We create our purpose based on our passion. We all have a passion for something; we all have skills, abilities readily available to be explored, and all we need to do is to get in touch with them and act. That much is simple, but it is important to understand that we do not know what is good or bad for other people and some could argue that it is not ideal to tell them what to do based on our convictions of what is good and what is not. That is equivalent to trying to help a fish by putting it safely up in a tree. The purpose of life is to be alive and enjoy the ride; there is no destination that we need to strive for, life simply 'is'.

I believe that we get too consumed by the news, advertisements, and propaganda – that we completely forget what is important and what is not. The media tells us every day what we should be concerned about. It tells us that without make-up we are not beautiful; that having a fat stomach makes us unattractive; that if we don't have an amazing car we shall feel incomplete (and therefore we shall work to have it); that if we don't dress to impress, we don't deserve respect; and that if we have not climbed the corporate ladder, we are less valuable than those who have. That is ridiculous, and the media constantly find ways to make us feel less valuable than others and not good enough.

We have forgotten that the most amazing things in life are free. We fight to live in a house with a garden and swimming pool, and we forget that we have a beach that is free to go to and a lot more fulfilling. We forget that what mother-nature offers us is a lot more beautiful – she is free and all we need.

*On The Road To Enlightenment*

I believe that the day we stop looking at our fellow human beings as competition but as brothers and sisters worthy of unconditional love regardless of the nature of their imperfections, we will live in a much better world. So my question today is: is there any hope for humanity?

# CHAPTER 15

# The Self

When I went to the monastery in Nepal, it was natural to ask others what had brought them there, what their purpose was and what they were looking for. One of the women at the retreat asked me what had brought me to the monastery, and my reply was, 'I came here to find myself'.

She looked at me and said, 'I am sorry to tell you this, but, apparently there is no such thing as self'.

Okay, that's depressing! How can it be that there is no self? Well, it was way too early for me to understand– I'm not sure if she tried to explain the concept to me but I wouldn't have been able to understand it yet even if she had. These notions are very difficult to put into words because fully understanding our nature is a realisation.

People tend to feel very attached to their personas. They have a strong ego and pride in their persona. They identify themselves with their ego or notion of the self–

they separate themselves from where they belong, and I wonder why they feel lonely? I wonder why they feel depressed easily? I wonder why they fight with one another? I wonder why they destroy our mother-nature? I wonder why they have a sense of emptiness?

As Hubert Reeves states beautifully, 'Man is the most insane species. He worships an invisible god and destroys a visible nature. Unaware that this nature he's destroying is this god he's worshipping'.

The word 'persona' comes from Latin 'mask'—a character played by an actor which originally referred to a theatrical mask. If we look closely at our behaviour, we shall conclude that we are always acting. There is no constant self. We behave differently towards our parents, certain family members, and towards our children. We behave differently towards our boss at work, our spouse, our colleagues at work, and towards the president and so forth. We are constantly acting; without realising it, we put on the mask and play a different role in relation to the situation and whom we are dealing with. With this in mind, the question could be: so who am I?

We could assume that we are the person who comes home and is alone with him—or herself. This conclusion could be valid, but it gets a bit tricky, because getting to know oneself is equivalent to biting one's own teeth—it is basically impossible. We are always in relation to someone else; we are all interconnected—there is no separate 'I'. If a tree falls in the desert and makes a sound, but no one is there to hear it, does it still make a sound? Sounds are produced by our ears, so if no one can hear, is there a sound?

It is important to remember that black implies white, life implies death, inside requires outside, yin and yang; one doesn't exist without the other. The same goes for human beings. We are not separate from one another – we are not separate from nature or the universe. We are one. We are the universe, just like the waves, mountains, trees, birds; everything is interconnected and one, cannot exist without the other.

Trying to separate oneself by letting the ego take over, believing we are special and unique, is not a very good idea. Connecting, however, with our true nature, without separating the 'I', and truly being with this nature is the secret to liberation. Once we do find liberation, interconnectedness, it will allow us to simply relax, let go, trust the universe, trust our nature, trust that once we eat our stomach will digest the food. We can trust that our body will breath without any commands. We can even trust our nervous system to the point that we can request it to wake us up at 7:00 a.m., and it will.

If you believe in the big bang theory, you shall understand that we are not a result of the big bang, but rather a part of it – part of the continuous process. What we do is what the universe is doing at the place we call 'here and now'. With this realisation we shall begin to be on good terms with our own being and to trust our brain.

## Chapter 16

## Do Humans Really Care as Much as They Say They Do?

I find it interesting that when speaking to others, people have a need or tendency to share their good deeds and find ways to show how they have evolved or are more compassionate than others. Actually I'm not sure if I find it interesting or if I worry about it indeed, as I have noticed that most people are not in connection with their true nature. They are basically unaware of their flaws, their selfish nature, and tend to put themselves on the pedestal while thinking everybody else needs to improve. Even when debating about religion, people who say they accept every religion and love them all do so with a sense of superiority as if 'I am better than you because I am fair and accept all religions fairly'.

I have noticed that some people lie about their emotions whether the emotion is hate, love, passion, or emotional dependency, because these emotions are normally perceived by society as a sign of weakness. If we are sad about something, we shall act as if we aren't because that is what society makes us do. Even if you are in love with someone, you shall act as if you aren't, otherwise you shall be perceived as the weak one in the pair–someone who will be stepped on, who the other person will feel too comfortable with and stop making the effort to make the relationship as amazing as it always has been.

Okay, so let's take a look at our nature, have you come to realise how selfish we are? Each of our acts is for our own benefit, which also includes the relationships we stay in as long as the partner maintains our ego boost. In other words, most people stay in relationships because of how the other person treats them, and the moment the partner stops treating them in a way that releases dopamine and makes them feel special, what do people do? Complain, put pressure on, and, if nothing changes, the person leaves the relationship because it no longer fulfils its purpose.

On a different note, let's assume you are giving money to the poor and nobody is watching, meaning that you are doing a good deed for yourself. We could conclude there is no ego boosting in this case, but let's also assume that the beggar, instead of giving a smile and saying thank you, takes the money and leaves. How do you feel about that? I will take a wild guess and suggest that you would probably be annoyed and not satisfied.

Why is that? Again, you did the good deed because you wanted the beggar to acknowledge it, and possibly smile and thank you. Would you call this pure kindness or are we back to our ego boosting?

Once my colleagues and I decided to give a donation to an orphanage located where all the waste is deposited in Maputo, so it's not the best place to go to and pretty uncomfortable. When we arrived a nun welcomed us, but she was not friendly at all; in fact, she criticised us for giving the orphans second-hand clothes. She had the guts to say that nowadays there were plenty of shops to buy clothes, and therefore they did not need our second-hand clothes and would burn them. We were very disappointed to see zero appreciation for the time we had dedicated to collect the donations! After that we went to another orphanage, which was much better than the previous one, and actually a very nice place to be. They welcomed us, thanked us in many ways, asked to take photos with us, and a while later we received a thank-you letter. Everything was really nice and made us feel truly special.

Let's take a look at both scenarios and the way they made me feel. The nun at the first orphanage was literally unkind and ungrateful, which made me feel down, whereas at the other orphanage I felt special, appreciated, and truly useful. The interesting question is, did I organise the donations because I cared or was it to be recognised and feed my ego? Both could have been motives, but the boosting of the ego continued to be one of the factors for my actions.

This is what I mean when I speak about selfishness. We are selfish, full stop, and everything we do revolves around our needs and the feelings our actions bring. Being selfish is not bad a thing at all, we need it for survival, but it would help if people were aware of their nature and fully understood their behaviour. I fully believe that once we realise our ulterior motives, we will become more aware of the ego and able to accept ourselves and others as fallible human beings, accept the world as unfair – simply accept.

*On The Road To Enlightenment*

## CHAPTER 17

## The Need to Belong

I often sit with women and they tell me that society's standards are unfair. For example, we shall have our hair neat, preferably straight or pulled back in any style other than an Afro.

I want to make very clear that I don't necessarily agree with how most things work, but rather accept how they work. Straight hair has been more fashionable lately and associated with seriousness, neatness, beauty, and responsibility, making African-looking people with ethnic hair feel cheated and unfairly treated. For them (I will speak in the third person) to feel like they belong and are widely accepted in the work environment, they must use chemicals on their hair or put a wig on – or resort to other methods that are very damaging to the hair.

Most people have adapted to this, but there are others who don't agree. I know a lawyer, for example, who was told she needed to adjust her hairstyle, which showed off her voluminous curls, to a more conventional hairstyle.

To be more specific, she was told to straighten her hair. This woman was approached by her HR manager who was concerned by her natural curls, which she loved by the way. I think these words will echo in her mind every time she looks in a mirror, which is not cool.

I myself have been struggling with this subject for quite some time. After going to Nepal I came back and I dressed in a hippie style. I thought I should do what I wanted, dress as I liked, and I didn't give any importance to what people thought. I believed that the way I thought and felt were more important than anything else. I went back to the corporate world. I managed a team, which meant being an example for my staff. As any human being–we have an inherit desire to belong–I wanted to feel pretty and appreciated. I wanted people to think that I was attractive and to see my credibility.

What does that mean? If I wanted to feel I belonged to society, accepted by society, and perceived in the ways I mentioned, I needed to look a certain way to fit in. Think about it? Before you become interested in engaging with someone or know anything deeper about them, the first impression is what counts, which fully involves physical appearance. If success within society is our goal, we must learn how to play the game. I have previously talked about our nature as personas, how we are not set in stone and how everything is an act. Dealing with society is just another act we put on, and this act is for our own benefit. What is of utmost importance is not the act itself but being aware that everything is an act.

Going back to the hair example, some may find the standards about straightening ethnic hair unfair, but this is how things work in society. I can complain about my unhappiness and express my disagreement, but things are the way they are and we all have a choice. You can start a revolution and dedicate your time and effort to getting things going. You can do what I did, which is to abandon the corporate world of working for someone else, living by their rules, and start your own business and live by your own rules instead. You can give up on society or become a hippie. You can change societies to one that resonates to your perspective. Or, if you are not willing to do any of that, you can accept your position and play the game fully. None of the paths are wrong, right, bad, or good. They are simply paths, and you have the power and right to choose what is best for you and what's in your best interest.

When I used to dress as a hippie, even though I was comfortable in my own skin, I no longer felt pretty, attractive, or perceived as attractive. This hindered my growth; it deeply influenced how people perceived and interacted with me. That may work for some, but it didn't work for me, and therefore I decided to play the game of life consciously. The day I become a well-known therapist and am recognised for

*Sharlene Sema Raston*

what I do – for my skills and professionalism – shall be the day I worry a lot less about appearances and fitting in.

# CHAPTER 18

# Our Nature

Who are we, and what is this mysterious experience we call life? Some people believe we came from the big bang, others that God created the world, and others say they have no idea. Whether you are a religious person or not, there may have been times when you have truly wondered. And regardless of how religious some people may be, and how much they claim to believe in any teaching, there is a degree of uncertainty in most of us about where we came from and what happens when we die. Have you noticed that even the most religious people who believe in heaven are not very keen to die even though they believe they will go to heaven?

Islam has five pillars, including:

> *a)* **Believing** and acknowledging that no one has the right to be worshiped except **Allah** (God) whose messenger is **Muhammad**, Performing

**Salat** (the obligatory prayers performed by Muslims five times a day),

b) Paying **Zakat** (giving money to the poor),

c) Fasting during **Ramadan** (the holy month), and

d) Going on **Hajj** (pilgrimage) once in your lifetime if you have the means to do so.

Like most religions, Islam also has spiritual teachings, but most people tend to focus on the commands above anything else. People may especially emphasise the command to not eat pork or drink alcohol. But I have witnessed many Muslims who don't drink alcohol to follow the commands, but smoke weed instead. Not eating pork is so stressed that a Muslim is more likely to drink alcohol than eat pork, and those who choose to eat pork are shunned. This is very interesting reasoning, which shows that the commands are also culture based. When I was at the university, when I would say that I couldn't eat pork, my friend would sarcastically reply, 'You can't eat pork, but you can drink?'. To her, my approach made absolutely no sense considering that drinking alters one's state and has many more disadvantages in comparison to eating pork. But most Muslims disagree with her view as far as I have observed.

Some people are indeed afraid of death. They don't understand it, and fear of the unknown is pretty natural. If we think about it, however, human beings by nature love impermanence and surprise, and, at the same time, we tend to give less value to something we have conquered that becomes permanent. It is as if once we know we have something, the magic goes away and we become interested in a new challenge instead. This is probably why marriages fall apart and the best part of the relationship is indeed when a couple is dating. Once people are married, all of the surprise, trying to impress and work on not losing the partner somehow become insignificant–partners grow accustomed to each other and slowly the passion goes away. With a deadline, most of us still have the tendency to procrastinate, and this applies to life, too. For us to be motivated to live it to the fullest, we shall remind ourselves that life is impermanent and one day we shall face death. Therefore, we should try our best to not only enjoy it but also spend more quality time with our significant others.

On a different note, the universe is vast, amazing, and full of beauty and magic. The older we get, the less we appreciate the beauty of the universe. Therefore, there is a need to bring new life again, to those who will fully appreciate its magic. Have you noticed how toddlers and children are amazed when they see simple things and try to share them with us by asking us to observe it, too? They show tremendous enthusiasm, whereas we tend to either act like we are also amazed by it, or we are honest, straightforward, and make it clear that we have seen it a thousand times. No, we are not amused by it. What amazes a child can be something as simple as an interesting insect or a rainbow.

*Sharlene Sema Raston*

Let's for a moment assume there is no death. First, the world would become overpopulated, unbearable, and fail to provide for everyone. People would reach the epitome of procrastination, as they literally would have all the time in

the world to get things done. The mystery of life would go away, and, as a result of the permanence of it, most people would appreciate life a lot less than they do now—giving even lesser meaning to it.

Adding to that, life is not the most amazing or easy thing in the world. At least human life has its challenges. Our feelings may be compared to a rollercoaster due to all the internal and external aspects that contribute to our emotional disturbances. Human beings are experts in causing themselves emotional disturbance with the lenses they use to interpret things and events; namely, their lack of tolerance to things, and high expectations with regards to the world and other people. These expectations may be demands about how the world should be, how things work, and how people behave and treat them. Or they may be related to infinite desires that have not been well thought out, leading to a degree of emptiness experienced by most people at different levels. None of these things are healthy and most definitely contributes to emotional disturbance.

As human beings become more and more developed, the greater is our hunger for instant gratification in order to achieve things. People often want the world to provide them with the things they want at the exact time they want them, and, when their desires aren't met, this leads to high levels of frustration and unhealthy negative emotions. It has come to a point that, on the very same note, people don't want to experience negative emotions. They fight them and somehow believe they 'shouldn't' feel that way. The bad news for us is, there is absolutely no way we will

not experience negative emotions at many stages of life. If someone dear to us dies, we should expect to grieve and feel sad. There is no positivistic theory that relieves those emotions because there is nothing great about losing someone.

But as I explained earlier, we should distinguish between healthy and unhealthy negative emotions. Instead of feeling depressed (unhealthy negative emotion), we should work towards feeling sad (healthy negative emotion). Healthy negative emotions are realistic and require insight based on how we perceive or interpret the situations which directly affect our emotional state and therefore our behaviour. It is very important for us to be fully aware of our own thoughts, as it all starts from there. Cultivating a healthy mind directly influences our lives and is a wise thing to do. That way we shall become the master of our minds, feelings, and behaviours, which is certainly in our best interest.

We do not have full control of our external circumstances or of events that happen out of the blue—we don't. We do, however, have the capacity to have full control of our perception of things and on whether we want to be miserable, feel sorry for ourselves, and perceive ourselves as puppets of fate and believe the universe is conspiring against us. Or we can understand and accept life as it is—accept that bad things happen to good people all the time, and that life is often not fair. Above all else, we can take responsibility for our actions and stop blaming circumstances and other people. How about we start becoming fully responsible for our choices, stop playing the victim and blaming the past for how things are at the moment, and be fully accountable for our past actions and acknowledge how they may have influenced the way things are today? Every new day we have an opportunity to do things differently and take steps that allow us to move in our chosen direction.

I find that many people tend to place too much emphasis on the past to explain their current behaviour and how things are. Or they tend to place their focus on the future and what they wish to attain, fully certain that once they get there, they will be completely happy. With regards to the past, I am going to make it very clear that there is no past: the past has vanished just like the wake of the ship vanishes. The wake of a ship tells us where the boat has been, but it does not drive the boat. In fact, the wake vanishes just like the past does.

I once shared an idea on Facebook that things are not explained by the past; they are explained by what happens now. A friend of mine disagreed, pointing to her experience of getting her degree later in life because when she was younger she didn't have the opportunity to do so. As Alan Watts says, 'Explaining things by the past is a refusal to explain things at all'. I replied that her explanation for how the past influenced her getting a degree in the present did not explain a thing, because what was relevant was knowing why she was doing it now. Many people don't have the opportunity to study when they are young, and when they have the means in their adulthood, many inevitably decide not to get a degree. In fact, the majority of people don't. There is no evidence of cause and effect in this particular subject, and she should have been looking at what was driving her decision in the here and now.

On a different note, as I stated previously, most people unconsciously or consciously chase happiness and fully believe that once they achieve certain things in life, they will be fully satisfied and happy. This causes a sense of scarcity, and the more people chase the things they think they lack, the emptier and poorer they feel—they perceive happiness as a destination, and it is not. In addition to that, once people achieve what they have been fighting for with the conviction that they will be happy, they can easily have a wake-up call and be disappointed. Then they realise that their wishes, desires, and this chasing mentality made them miss everything that happened along the way because they believed there was a golden goodie at the end of the line.

*Sharlene Sema Raston*

Life should not be perceived as a destination at which to arrive. Life is this, the here and now, which is all we have at the moment. Therefore, we shall be aware and realise that the golden goodie is not at the end of the line; it has been here all along and we didn't realise it. Many women, for example, dream about getting married and fully believe that once they do, they shall feel fully complete and find ultimate happiness. I've never understood this train of thought as it is pretty obvious that the happiness levels within a marriage are not great: with marriage comes great responsibility and many conflicts which need dedication, patience, willingness, and so forth to resolve. And there is absolutely no evidence that once a woman gets married she shall be at the peak of happiness. The women who do have this conviction spend most of their lives not living to the fullest, but worried about being married and working hard to attain it. Once they marry, they realise it is not all that—just like everything in life that has its challenges, so does being married. Then a wife may look back and have a sense of regret because she did not live or enjoy life to the fullest while chasing this illusion of end-of-the-line happiness.

In my therapy sessions, I once asked one of my clients to describe what would it take her to be happy. She described getting married, starting a family, having a perfect and stable marriage, and so forth. In other words, she described a utopia. Waiting for all of these conditions to exist to be happy is a recipe for a disaster, as there will never be full enjoyment in life as long as happiness is associated with something else. On the other hand, starting a family is not a guarantee of happiness because there are plenty of unhappy married people. This is to highlight the importance of the here and now, the importance of being grounded, the importance of staying where we are and come to realisations to become more conscious and awake to all of the things we create to block our own happiness.

## Chapter 19

## My Experience as a Therapist

Cognitive behavioural therapy, especially rational emotive behavioural therapy, is a structured, goal-oriented therapy in which ideally the therapist and the client focus on one goal and work towards it during the treatment period. The idea is to know before each session what shall be done and follow the designed structure. In real life the approach does not work this way, because clients are unstable. In my experience, many things happen during the therapeutic process that make it impossible to follow the structure. Often by the time clients come to the next session, they have a brand-new issue they want to work on or a change in perspective. After dealing with many clients, I came to the realisation that I needed to adapt my therapy skills to benefit the client and his or her needs. Some clients love the practicality of my approach. They love the fact that they don't need to speak about their childhood unless necessary, they love not having to get into too much detail regarding their personal lives, and they love the fact that it is a behavioural-focused type of therapy, which means it is focused on action and putting things into practice.

I once had a client who did not believe in therapy but really enjoyed our sessions. She shared her experience with her husband, and he, too, was curious to try. What he told me was, 'My wife loved you very much, as she said that you completely dismiss the past'. My approach shocked him, and I was relatively surprised because I don't even give it a second thought. It is the most natural way to work because I don't believe in the past. In fact, when clients try to justify things by pointing to the past, I quickly tell them that the past is irrelevant at this stage. What has happened may have contributed to how things are at this stage, but I am interested in understanding why clients behave the way they do today. As I mentioned, explaining things by the past is a complete refusal to explain things at all.

On another note, I do have clients that truly enjoy speaking and sharing their thoughts and views, and therefore I have started adapting my therapy style to them by listening and asking the questions that will lead them to their own truth and the answers they seek. I can understand and see the importance of having someone listening to you—to listen to your ideas and experiences without interruption or the need for judgement.

I have mentioned these examples to point out that pure CBT/REBT is not for everyone; indeed, it is only for some people. Having an integrative approach normally works better because it is more flexible and takes into account the variety of clients and their different needs. I have found that borrowing concepts, ideas, and approaches from different therapies may be much more beneficial than focusing on one therapy style alone. Of course, I never borrow concepts that go against the core of my beliefs or therapy style, but choose those that compliment my style.

People don't really need therapists if they do the job on their own. Simply by learning the relevant material and perspectives, they can easily become their own therapists. But often people are not very interested in such an investment and don't prioritise it or dedicate time to it. To learn Eastern philosophy, infinite reading material and videos are readily available for free on the internet. However, laziness and a lack of understanding the importance of focusing on self-development keeps people stuck, so that they tend to associate negative events with unluckiness and fully ignore their accountability as to why things are the way they are. I shall be fully honest that psychoeducation is an absolute requirement to overcome any difficult period or to live a healthier and fulfilled life. If one is concerned with that, some dedication to psychoeducation is crucial. It may sound like a catch-22, because the vast amount of relevant and irrelevant information available on the internet may lead to confusion. An important skill to develop is to be able to select the material carefully and focus on the wise, applicable, and relevant material that may lead to enlightenment.

In the doctrine of Buddhism, it is essential to find a guru, or teacher, who shall guide the student and help him or her in the quest for enlightenment. The choice of teacher is a crucial aspect as the student will absorb the teachings it is important to choose with diligence. In the same way, this diligence should be used when selecting online material. Ask yourself: what is my perspective of life, or what perspective resonates most with me? What do I want? Where do I want to go? What is my goal in life? Whose work do I fully admire? What qualities do I admire and who possesses such qualities that I can use as a form of inspiration?

If you haven't found what you're looking for yet, keep looking and you shall find. There are plenty of teachers out there, and you have access to their teachings in the form of YouTube videos for free. You can either choose to continuously learn from your mistakes only, or to learn from others too, which minimises the chances of making unnecessary mistakes. The Buddhist perspective has been the most enlightening one for me, but it is not exclusive. We can learn greatly from Hare Krishna, from Hinduism, Taoism, Islam, Christianity, Judaism, Bahá'í Faith—from any great Western teacher or successful entrepreneur who inspires, such as Richard Branson.

As a philosopher from a very young age, I had the opportunity to be exposed to various philosophical theories and philosophers. And at first, I found that each philosophical perspective was so well explained and argued that I would easily follow. But then, I would learn about a different and opposite one that was equally well formulated and argued, and I would follow that one, too, and this process continued until I managed to formulate my own theory that fully resonated with me. It took the course of many years, of changes accompanied by growth and understanding, but I can finally say that I have a strong and grounded perspective and opinion on things. I have realised that I can learn from all corners and that each corner has valuable knowledge – including religions. By fully engaging with some belief systems, I have found that their knowledge and teachings do not oppose each other but simply complement one another.

At the beginning of my journey as a philosopher, I once read, 'When you study philosophy superficially you tend to move away from God or even stop believing in the concept. When you get deeper into it you tend to move closer to God and get a deeper understanding of it.' I read it many years ago and obviously do not remember the exact words but the essence is there. Even though there is much criticism of and some negative aspects about religion, to be against religion is to have not yet transcended.

## Chapter 20

## Religion and Religious Beliefs

I come from a Muslim background and I have a good understanding of Islam. I had also been exposed to Christianity and reading some chapters of the Bible has helped me to understand some of its concepts. In 2012, I went to Nepal for a retreat which allowed me to become more familiar with Buddhism; and I later learnt more about Hinduism and Hare Krishna. These latter religions are often misunderstood; they are truly precious, and there is much beauty and wisdom in them. One of my closest and best friends at the university was of the Bahá'í Faith, so I also had the privilege of learning and being part of that group. The conclusion I have reached is that the essence of most religions is very similar; all of them complement one another. Thanks to all of them, I can reach a better understanding of things and understand the unity concept.

People are often so busy defending their religion and views that they don't genuinely interact with other religions and try to understand. But genuine dialogue leads to the

realisation that there is absolutely no need to turn religion into a competition. It is not productive nor wise for human beings to separate from one another, and to elevate our beliefs in relation to others. We should simply try to learn from one another because it makes us wiser. Then we can realise that the essence of religions is similar, presented in different ways only to bring the sense of 'us' versus 'them'.

When we are born, many things are determined for us– our name, nationality, race group, religion, beliefs, and so forth—and we dedicate most of our lives defending as the ultimate truth these concepts and ideas that have been imposed on us from childhood. They are not something we choose but something that have been imposed on us. This goes for atheists, too, who often believe that they have come up with their views on their own and are therefore more rational than others. But in fact the majority of them come from a circle of atheists.

When it comes to religion, the greatest disadvantage is that the rulers tend to twist religious beliefs to their own advantage, be it political or social. There have been evidences that men have made changes to the scriptures to bene- fit themselves and create more control over people. I tend to not trust people in power or their genuine intentions, because they want to be in control. On the other hand, I also don't believe the scriptures are completely adulterated. Therefore, I do my best to take the most important things that make sense to me and ignore the rest. As the Buddha once said, we shall always analyse information and the things shared with us to make sure they make rational sense to us—even his own teachings. An interesting fact about Siddhartha Gautama (the Buddha) is that he did not teach all communities in the same way. He presented his teachings using different metaphors, according to the group, their culture, and their way of viewing things. Because there is no such thing as one size fits all, adaptation is very important. As an example, with a certain community he might use the concepts of heaven and hell because they resonate with this community, whereas he wouldn't introduce these terms as a metaphor to other communities. This shows his flexibility and reinforces the idea that the essence of religion is the same, and only its presentation is different.

My last engagement with religion had been with Buddhism, and I have delved deeper into its teachings. In some sense Mahayana Buddhism lost its philosophical only aspect and became too dogmatic. Some of the masters would instil fear in their followers, highlighting the fact that we shall end up in hell. They taught that we shall improve ourselves out of fear of going to hell—in other words, of being reborn into a lower realm. When I got into those teachings, it was indeed off-putting to me. I do, however, love the Mahayana tradition and I have learnt much from it and shall continue to do so.

*Sharlene Sema Raston*

Human beings are those responsible for changing the meaning of religion, and, as a result, being selective about the information exposed to us is very important. There are some other concepts in Buddhism, mostly in the Mahayana tradition, that do not resonate with me, including the constant prostrations to the Buddha statue and to masters, or gurus, and offerings of water, food, and incense to the Buddha statues. I am also not sure how accurate the wheel of life or the realms are, as there is no way to verify that. I would guess that other perspectives, such as Zen would be more spiritual, more focused on emptiness, more detached, and fully aimed at enlightenment in a different, flexible, and free way—I am imagining, of course.

When I was at the monastery in Nepal, I talked with the nuns about the fact that I can relate to Buddhism but there is one factor that didn't resonate with me—I believe in God, and the Buddhist perspective does not. One nun told me that there was nothing wrong with that, it was perfectly fine, but that as I dove deeper into my search there would come a stage that the beliefs related to the perspective of God would clash. Six years later I have found that the beliefs have clashed, so I have developed my own perspective of things in which I shall not be committed to any of the religions but continuously combine them to form my own views. This includes the monotheistic religions, which are rich in knowledge.

I was impressed by the Hindu concepts and perspective of things—that we all have the divine within us and are therefore perceived as gods, that we should fully respect and value all sentient beings, and the concept that the world is perceived as play and therefore we shall not take things too seriously. I also love how Hindus are so concerned about life that they often choose to become vegetarians. I perceive it as a beautiful, practical, and down-to-earth religion that preaches respect and caring for Mother Nature.

I've mentioned the fact that most of us are given a name, religion, and so forth when we are born and that we usually spend the rest of our lives defending these ideas. This may give us the impression that we have chosen our path, when actually indoctrination has had a huge impact on our beliefs. Before Siddhartha Gautama became the Buddha, he used to be a prince—and he used to be Hindu. Even though he went on a quest to find his own truth, he had already been indoctrinated with Hindu beliefs. If we take a look at Buddhism, we can find many similarities with Hinduism, and therefore even though he consciously and unconsciously came up with his own theories regarding suffering and an understanding of the world, his approach was highly influenced by his previous beliefs. We as human beings cannot really come up with new ideas that we haven't already been exposed to—and Hinduism was all Siddhartha knew. I could suggest that if he had been exposed to Judaism instead, there is huge probability that his approach would have been different—maybe even a monotheistic approach. Indoctrination plays a major role in our spiritual path. Have you noticed that we are only able to imagine what we have seen and experienced? Take a look at people's descriptions of what heaven looks like. They tend to describe the most amazing mundane things: heaven with stunning rivers, fruit, and beauty all around, and hell with hellfire. When we want to draw an angel, the image we have is a beautiful person with wings, while the devil is normally associated with horns. Our imagination is limited, and what people don't realise is that all those ideas of beauty in paradise or hellfire are only applicable if we are human beings. They tend to forget that once we die, what decomposes is our body, so there shall be no physical body in the afterlife to have those experiences unless God gives us another body. On the same note, being human also implies many annoying aspects (such as hunger, thirst, bowel movements, sickness, tiredness…) that I don't believe would go hand-in-hand in heaven. If there is such thing as heaven, I believe we shall carry a different form that is compatible with the universe we will be at. It is important to remember that the human-being form is in relation to this world and applicable to it, too.

We live in one of many galaxies. And planet earth is not the only planet that has the conditions to create life—there are many other planets similar to planet earth in that respect. What type of life could there be on other planets? Which forms? How do they do things? We cannot imagine those things, as they are beyond our human capacity. And even though the planets have potential to support life, this does not necessarily imply human life, which requires very specific conditions.

Before people decided to go to space, the idea was that heaven was in the sky. I believe that many people still hold to this belief even though they know there is nothing in the sky. This could be a metaphor to say that heaven is on another planet somewhere in space. Heaven and hell, if they do exist, must be somewhere, and they could be located on other planets indeed. In Islam it is said that there is a hierarchy in heaven. In other words, there are seven heavens from the lowest to the highest heaven, which is called Jannat Firdous. This is where we all wish to go, where all of the prophets are located; it is as close to God as a being can ever be. In my humble opinion these ideas are interconnected with the idea of life on other planets.

Based on many different teachings and perspectives, there is some consensus in acknowledging Jesus of Nazareth as one of the most predominant prophets that came to earth— others perceive him as the son of God or God himself who came to earth to save us. He was very special in many ways and also had the power to perform miracles, such as transforming water into wine. Someone once posted on social media that it was impressive that during his adulthood Jesus managed to have twelve very close friends, which were obviously his disciples, and someone commented on the post that if he had a friend who could turn water into wine, he would definitely make sure to stay friends with that person—best friends. The birth of Jesus Christ through a virgin, which is supported by the Koran, was also a miracle. And Jesus was the only messenger who died and was resuscitated.

Christians believe that Jesus of Nazareth was resuscitated, whereas Muslims claim that when the Jews went to look for him to kill him, God elevated Jesus to heaven and replaced him with someone else of the same image. So Muslims do not believe that Jesus was resuscitated, but they agree that he will return to earth just before the day of judgement. On the other hand, Jews do not believe that Jesus was the Messiah, which explains the fact that he was killed and accused of blasphemy. The Jews are still waiting for the Messiah to come, whereas Christians and Muslims are waiting for his second appearance to fulfil what has been written in the scriptures. I see consistency in the teachings in terms of Jesus coming back to earth, with the differences related to the circumstances of when this will happen and the purpose or meaning of it.

All religions appear to be interconnected. For example, Hindus perceive us as gods who have the divine within. Passages in the scriptures support this idea in both the Old Testament and the New Testament.

In Psalm 82 (The New International Version), it states: 4Rescue the weak and needy; deliver them out of the hand of the wicked.

5They know nothing, they understand nothing

They walk about in darkness; all the foundations of the earth are shaken.

6"I said, 'You are "gods";

You are all sons

of the Most High'.

7But you will die like mere men;

you will fall

like every other ruler"

8Raise up, O God, judge the earth, for all the nations

are your inheritance.

And John 10 (The New International Version)

31Again the Jews picked up stones to stone him, 32but Jesus said to them, "I have shown you many great miracles from the father. For which of these do you stone me?"

33"We are not stoning you for any of these," replied the Jews, "but for blasphemy, because you, a mere man, claim to be God".

34Jesus answered them, "Is it not written in your Law, 'I have said you are gods'? If he called the 'gods', to whom the word of God came-and the Scripture cannot be broken- 36what about the one whom the Father set apart as his very own and sent into the world? Why then do you accuse me of blasphemy because I said, 'I am God's son? 37Do not believe me unless I do what my father does. 38But if I do it, even though you do not believe me, believe the miracles, that you may know and understand that the Father is in me, and I in the Father."

Based on the passages above we may conclude that Jesus may share the Hindu perspective that we all have the divine within us, and what appears to be happening in Christianity is that its followers only recognised the divine within Jesus and not anyone else. In other words, they make divinity exclusive to Jesus. Yet Jesus says we are all children of God. In other words, it is not exclusive to him.

# CHAPTER 21

# Self-Reflections

I perceive life as an interesting phenomenon, because the law of nature seems to follow the same pattern in all aspects. Have you realised that no human being has everything or is completely happy? There is always something important lacking in people's lives that they have decided has tremendous value, which blocks them from feeling happy and fulfilled. Even if they have most things in abundance, you find that they suffer from unexplained depression or another mental condition that hinders them from living a happy and fulfilled life.

As an example, a very rich person may have all the financial fortune in the world but lack in family relations – or that person may have a good family bond, but then life compensates by giving him or her poor health. You may also find a poor person who lacks in economic resources but has a strong family bond and support system, which contributes greatly to their level of happiness.

*Sharlene Sema Raston*

In Northern Europe, people may have absolutely everything and enjoy a great lifestyle, but the weather is miserable. They are not lucky enough to have warm days throughout the year, such as in most countries in Africa. Africa is a poor continent, in general, but on the other hand the sun is always out, the weather is nice and warm, the Indian Ocean is near, which is nice and warm, and people normally share the mindset of *ubuntu*, which means, I am because we are. As opposed to Europe where most people are individualistic and there is very little cohesion, Africans share a sense of togetherness, love for one another, and goodwill towards their neighbour. People therefore tend to have a higher sense of security because if they ever need anything, they can literally count on most people to be there for them. For example, someone who is broke and cannot afford to buy food may easily go to a friend's house, a family member's house, and that person shall be genuinely welcomed in for a meal. Families are a lot bigger and closer to one another, unlike most countries in Europe where families are normally a lot smaller. This lack of closeness contributes greatly to loneliness and an individualistic way of being.

There is a very interesting phenomenon I noticed while chatting with some people – namely, an American friend of mine who was twenty-seven years old at the time and was already saving money for retirement. I hadn't ever heard of young adults in Mozambique thinking so far in advance or worrying about such things – that thought was basically non-existent and I couldn't really argue with it. Could it be that the African mindset of not planning for tomorrow and just living each day, plus the lack of ambition that most people share, directly influences the fact that the continent is underdeveloped? I guess we trust in nature to provide and we really lack the ambition to accumulate fortunes, placing importance on factors such as family, social relations, time to relax, and precious time with loved ones.

For someone to be successful from the society's perspective, it normally involves working very hard, working longer hours, making work a priority, and in a way neglecting other things in life to be successful. The corporate ladder can be pretty hectic if your aim is to reach the top levels and compete. Another interesting characteristic of Mozambique specifically is that people don't tend to be serious competitors. This has a direct influence on the effort they put in their career or job, and, when combined with a lack of ambition, they may easily have poorer job performance in relation to other countries where people tend to be more competitive and highly ambitious. An advantage of the non-competitive mindset is that it makes it much easier to work as a team and to share the success. In Mozambique, you may easily find that if a friend is well-off at any stage, his or her tendency may be to share wealth with others, valuing interactions and togetherness as opposed to the financial side of things. Note that this is not set in stone. I am not suggesting that all people are like that. I am making a comparison of countries in Africa to more individualistic countries as our giving tendencies are more widespread.

I had to literally move to London and experience this lifestyle first-hand—the poor relationships between people, lack of friends, difficulty developing strong bonds with people, and loneliness—to come to the conclusion that I can be in a beautiful place, where everything works to a certain extent, a place full of opportunities and countless things to do and places to go to, but if I am alone, it brings no sense of happiness. I have learnt that in every situation there are advantages and disadvantages, and our decisions in life shall be dependent on what hardships are we willing to endure and what our values are.

I am not very keen to suffer every day in the cold, or take an hour to go to work and another hour to get back, or not have time to have a proper relaxed and flexible social life, so that it's a struggle to form strong bonds with others and it's a mission to be with or visit a friend. I'm not keen on all the struggles related to proper accommodation and privacy, the annoyance of going to the supermarket in the cold and walking back home with heavy plastic bags, to go out in the evening and have lots of fun, but to struggle to get back home late at night due to the lack of transport. Sometimes it would take me almost two hours to get home, and I would be exhausted and sleepy and still need to walk from the bus station or underground to get home in freezing weather.

All of these aspects about London and many more contribute to my preference to live elsewhere. On the other hand, Mozambique is underdeveloped. It is one of the poorest countries in the world with a terrible economy; the currency was devalued in 2015 and the price of goods doubled. This had an enormous negative effect on the economy. Mozambique hardly produces anything, and therefore we need to import all of our goods from overseas. Having our currency devalued meant that the price for the products got very high and guess what? The salaries stayed the same, and many lost their job as most companies reduced staff to cut costs. Mozambique is a very beautiful country; it has natural stunning beauty and awesome beaches. I enjoy the essence of Mozambicans, who are genuinely good people.

In many countries like South Africa, for example, people may be resentful about the countries or people who colonised them, tending to discuss this topic on such a regular basis, continuously playing the victim. On the other hand, there are also countries like England where people tend to have a very negative concept with regards to immigration. In this case, they are taking measures to reduce the immigration influx by having more control over their borders through Brexit. The immigration influx has been so high that England is becoming overpopulated, which directly affects the quality of the services, availability of jobs, distribution of resources, not to mention the great number of illegal immigrants.

In Mozambique people hardly complain about the colonial times, nor do they show any resentment towards the Portuguese. In fact if you ask any Mozambican what period they prefer the most, you shall find that the majority say, the colonial times. Many people in Mozambique are nostalgic for the colonial times, which they say had great advantages – the country was well-kept, there were great improvements, most material for building houses was of high quality, and the education was great. It was basically a lovely country in all aspects. When it comes to immigration, Mozambicans love immigrants and make them feel welcome.

Inhambane is one of the provinces in the south of Mozambique. It is known as *terra da boa gente*, which means, the land of good people; it is one of the most preferred provinces in Mozambique due to the breathtaking beaches, awesome vibe, and kind and friendly people. My sister once said that a German colleague of hers at the University of Cape Town mentioned that the people were so nice that if you imagine the friendliest person in Germany, the people from Inhambane were still nicer.

When it comes to serious career growth, self-development, continuous learning, health care, and education, Mozambique does lack. If you do want to provide a good education to your child, you should send him or her to one of the international schools. There is not much room for higher education, and therefore most people tend to go overseas. If you do want to have access to a good hospital, it is costly. The gap between the rich and the poor is large, and it is definitely in your best interest to be relatively wealthy if you live in Mozambique.

## Conclusion

I have tackled many different subjects, thoughts, and perspectives and you may realise that at times I may have exaggerated on my approach to things.

I want to make it clear that I am merely doing it for the sake of making a point and whatever it has been said throughout the book should be taken with some balsamic vinegar, olive oil, salt, pepper, and honey.

I have written this book based on the knowledge that I have learnt over the years, and further research is recommended to gain better or more accurate understanding regarding any of the ideas presented.

The purpose of this book is not for you to either agree with me or follow me but to simply make you think so you can decide things for yourself.

There are plenty of perspectives, cultures, religions, and traditions and I fully don't believe that one single attitude can objectively be perceived as the best; this would be equivalent as stating that Paracetamol shall be the cure for all illnesses, which is not realistic even though many people may not agree. We shall choose our medicine based on our condition which is profoundly influenced by some factors.

People tend to separate from each other for many reasons, and I shall tell you that, after working with plenty of people from different backgrounds, cultures, religions and so forth, I can guarantee you that we are all part of the same race – the human race. You will be very surprised to find that we all have the same fears, insecurities, wishes... We all want the same things; we want to be happy and experience the least discomfort that we possibly can.

If we do decide to unite as opposed to let our ego take the best of us, we will give us the opportunity to learn from each other and possibly come to the conclusion that all knowledge from all spheres is relevant to help us shape our thoughts more profoundly.

*Namaste!*

*Sharlene Sema Raston*

# Biography

I was born in Harare, Zimbabwe and soon after I moved to Maputo, Mozambique. I studied at the Portuguese school in Maputo, and in 2004 I moved to Pretoria, South Africa. I am a Cognitive Behavioral Therapist and Hypnotherapist and have been a registered Psychometrist (PMT 0086835) with the Health Professions Council of South Africa since 2011.

I completed my Honors Degree in Psychology at the University of South Africa (UNISA) and my Bachelor's degree at the University of Pretoria where I specialized in Psychology and Criminology. I completed a Diploma in the various Treatments and Effects of Addictions at the Open College University in the United Kingdom and own a certificate in Basic principles for First Line Managers from UNISA, SA.

My Psychometric training was carried out through UNISA; I gained a vast amount of knowledge while working at Momentum in Centurion and got accreditations for the Personal Profile Analysis tool (PPA) at Thomas International, Cognitive Process Profile tool (CPP) at Cognadev and the Learning Potential Computerised Adapt (LPCAT) developed by Marie De Beer.

I have many years of experience in the corporate world in Management in the Telecommunications Industry and Psychometric Testing. In 2016, I went to London to undergo training in Cognitive Behavioural Hypnotherapy at the UK College of Hypnosis and Hypnotherapy, one of the world's leading accredited hypnotherapy schools specializing in an evidence-based approach. I had also trained in Rational Emotive Behavioural Therapy (REBT) at the CCBT College in London, which is a pioneering form of Cognitive Behavioural Therapy (CBT) developed by Albert Ellis. For my Continuous Learning Development, I had the privilege to attend some seminars from Windy Dryden who is one of the leading practitioners and trainers in the UK in CBT and the first Briton to be accredited in REBT at the Albert Ellis Institute. The fundamental notion about REBT is that it is not the events that happen in our lives that disturb us, but the belief that we hold about the event that disturbs us, in other words, we disturb ourselves.

I follow the CBT approach, and my work is highly inspired by notorious figures such as the Buddha, Alan Watts, Albert Ellis, Aaron Beck, Windy Dryden, Victor Frankl and many more. As a result, I have combined the knowledge and training I had acquired over the years from the great philosophical thinkers into developing my unique view and perspective.

I will always refer to my present job as play because I wholeheartedly love what I do and at no given moment feel like I am working. I truly love my clients; I see a side of them that is so real, true, raw, and human. In society, everybody is too busy acting like the most influential human being on earth, cold, putting on a mask to chase success—trying to hide their emotions so as not be perceived as weak. It gets to a point that we can no longer know someone for real, due to the mask everyone constantly wears. In the therapy room the mask falls off completely, and I see people's real selves. I manage to see a human being in front of me, and I love it.

My passion for philosophy has been alive from the moment I was exposed to it at the school where I was known as Descartes. Moreover, I have now taken my first step towards my dream of becoming a writer.

## **Acknowledgments**

I would like to express special thanks to my wonderful and loving parents, Selma Ismael Sema and Roodolf Raston. They have guided me and helped me from the day I was born and whose kindness, love and care over the years is impossible to repay—you are irreplaceable; to my fantastic sister, Sharon Sema Raston, thank you for your endless support and love. I deeply value your guidance and care.

I would like to express my gratitude to my dearest cousins, Shirley Drost —thank you very much for your precious time reviewing my work and for the valuable and constructive feedback provided, I fully appreciate it.

To my family and friends, thank you for your support, inspiration and unconditional love.

Lastly, but perhaps most importantly, I would like to give a special thanks to God, the Almighty, for putting such amazing people in my life and for all the doors and opportunities that have been opening throughout my life.

This book is in memory of Alan Wilson Watts, whom I perceive to be one the greatest philosophers of all times and the one who had the most substantial impact in my current work and in shaping my ideas. I would like to celebrate his existence, celebrate his immortality, his wisdom and how lucky we are that he left amazing

*Sharlene Sema Raston*

amount of great works that we can all benefit from and had inspired me profoundly on many of the ideas presented throughout the book. As he once said: "All those stars, if you look out in the skies, is a fireworks display, like you see on the 4th of July, which is a great occasion for celebration. The universe is a celebration. It is a fireworks show to celebrate that existence is."

*Sharlene Sema Raston*